LEOPARDS
OF THE AFRICAN PLAINS

Katherine Walden

PowerKiDS press™

New York

For Bridget, Maeve, Margaret, and Danny Cook

Published in 2009 by The Rosen Publishing Group, Inc.
29 East 21st Street, New York, NY 10010

First Edition

Editor: Amelie von Zumbusch
Book Design: Erica Clendening
Layout Design: Julio Gil
Photo Researcher: Jessica Gerweck

Photo Credits: Cover, pp. 5, 7, 9, 11, 15, 17, 19, 21, 23, 24 (top right, bottom left, bottom right) Shutterstock.com; pp. 13, 24 (top left) © Beverly Joubert/Getty Images.

Library of Congress Cataloging-in-Publication Data

Walden, Katherine.
  Leopards of the African plains / Katherine Walden.— 1st ed.
    p. cm. — (Safari animals)
  Includes index.
  ISBN-13: 978-1-4358-2690-8 (library binding)— ISBN 978-1-4358-3064-6 (pbk.)
ISBN 978-1-4358-3076-9 (6-pack)
  1. Leopard—Africa—Juvenile literature. I. Title.
  QL737.C23W315 2009
  599.75'54096—dc22
                                    2008019536

Manufactured in the United States of America

CONTENTS

Leopards are large members of the cat family. They are beautiful and strong.

5

Leopards have **rosettes** on their backs. They have **spots** on their legs, faces, and fronts.

Many leopards live on Africa's **savannas**. A leopard's coat makes it hard to see against the savanna grasses.

Adult leopards live alone. Each leopard has its own territory, or land where it lives and hunts.

Leopard **cubs** live with their mothers for one or two years. Leopard mothers take good care of their cubs.

Leopards are very good at climbing. They are excellent jumpers, too.

15

Leopards are often found in trees. These cats climb trees to sleep, stay safe, and look for food.

Leopards are hunters. They use their sharp teeth to catch other animals for food.

Leopards creep up on the animals they are hunting. They are quiet and move carefully.

Leopards eat many animals, such as antelopes, zebras, rabbits, fish, and monkeys.

Words to Know

cub

rosettes

savanna

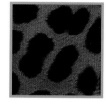

spots

Index

Web Sites

Due to the changing nature of Internet links, PowerKids Press has developed an online list of Web sites related to the subject of this book. This site is updated regularly. Please use this link to access the list:
www.powerkidslinks.com/safari/leopard/